WHAT CAN YOU SAY ABOUT GOD?*

*(Except God.")

What Can You Say About God?*

*(Except "God.")

by

William A. Luijpen

Translated by

Henry J. Koren, C.S.Sp.

PAULIST PRESS
New York / Paramus / Toronto

Library of Congress
Catalog Card Number: 76-171103

Published by Paulist Press
Editorial Office: 304 W. 58th St., N. Y., N. Y. 10019
Business Office: 400 Sette Drive, Paramus, N. J. 07652

Printed and bound in the
United States of America

Contents

Introduction

The purpose of this short book is to defend the relative "unimportance" of "learning" with respect to faith in God. It tries to show that a certain form of "thoughtlessness" is reasonable—the "thoughtlessness" which refuses to exchange authentic life for "learned" discourse. I find it "more important" that people know how to move around "intelligently" in time and space than that they understand the definition of space and time; more important that they try to be just than that they are able to philosophize about justice; more important that they practice the prayer of petition than that they endeavor to make the distinctions which theology tries to find in order to justify the meaning of such prayer.

"Good God! How awfully complicated is all this!" That's the sigh of many people who try to become acquainted with all the modern ideas about belief in God that are being circulated in our time. Much of what is being written today hardly amounts to more than intellectual gymnastics, but precisely when books and articles rise above this level, that sigh is very appropriate. "Do things have to be that difficult?" many a weary reader wonders.

It is indeed very difficult to dwell in the "house of learning," of explicit rationality, when this learning speaks "about" God. But the "house of learning" is not the "house of faith." This is what I'd like to show here. It is badly needed for someone to do it, for in our West Christian faith has gradually been reduced to a "yes" to "learned" statements. The question, however, is how important such a "yes" is.

For several decades now philosophy has been involved in an endeavor "to go back to reality itself." Today, theology also is hesitatingly entering this road "back." The results of this endeavor can be found in "learned" books. I'll not trouble my readers with them, although I have made use of them in writing this little work. One can convince himself of this matter by having a look at the bibliography appended to this book. But all these "learned" books are nothing but a laborious search for, and a partial discovery of, the insight that faith and "learning" are *not* identical. I'll be satisfied with the reception of this book if I can manage to show this to its readers.

Calling the Name "God"

What is it that the man of faith, the religious man, means when he calls the name "God"? There are people who in all sincerity think that there shouldn't be any believers in God, any religious people. Similarly, there are people who are convinced that there shouldn't be any artists. But, undeniably, there are artists. I may and even must therefore ask what an artist intends when he creates a work of art. For there cannot be any doubt that the artist intends something, even if some people are convinced that he should not intend anything. The same applies to the man of faith. He intends something when he calls the name "God," even though others are convinced that the man of faith has no right to exist. Whether we like it or not, the believer does exist. So, what does he mean when he calls "God"?

Let us note in the first place that the believer does indeed intend to *call* the name "God." He doesn't intend to "establish" that God exists, to "describe" what God is, or to "explain" anything by accepting God's existence. The religious man *calls* the name "God," and this "calling" can be a shouting, a whispering of his name. It can be a prayer, a song, an alleluia, a complaining, a sorrowing, a cursing: God! Thank God! God be praised! God Almighty! Goddamn!

When matters are expressed in this way, it should be evident that any interpretation of what it means to *call* the name of "God" should steer away from the idea that there is question here of "establishing" or "describing" "something" or "somebody," or that an attempt is made to "explain" "something by means of something" or "somebody by means of somebody."

When the believer calls, shouts or whispers the name "God," he expresses the mystery of his existence. Under certain conditions he discovers in his existence a "depth" whose "reality" cannot be indicated in "flat descriptive" terms functioning as particularizations of what in common parlance we call "something" or "somebody." In calling the name "God," the religious man doesn't intend to describe "something" or "somebody" just as he can describe a geological layer or John. Let us give a few examples:

A child is born, and the believer exclaims "God!"
In health or illness that believer shouts "God!"
He sexually unites with anther person and in his ecstasy the believer calls "God!"
He is dying and his lips whisper "God!"
At the rising and the setting of the sun, in the pale

light of the moon and the stars, before the roaring of the sea, at the undulating of the wheat stalks, the threat of a storm and the menace of a flood, at the welling up of a spring and the germinating of the seed, the believer exclaims "God!"

When he conquers in battle or suffers defeat, when he lives in poverty or in prosperity, when he suffers injustice or finds justice, the religious man calls "God!"

When he is reduced to slavery in Egypt, rises against his oppressors and when he overcomes the terrible risk of his revolt against his masters, the believer exclaims "God!"

When, while wandering through the desert with his people, he meets ethical demands imposing themselves on him as inescapable conditions of humanity, the religious man shouts "God!"

When he can finally establish himself in a land of his own, the believer calls "God!"

When he must go into exile, he complains "God!"

And when he can again return from his exile, he joyfully shouts "God!"

The religious man calls, shouts, whispers the name "God!" He prays and sings, he shouts for joy and laments, he sorrows and curses.

Situations of Existence

To understand what the believer means when he calls the name "God," one must conceive the above-mentioned situations as situations of existence, that is to say, as situations of *man,* viewed as an existent subject. This point must be stressed, for it is possible to speak about man without conceiving "man" as existent subject and, consequently, without conceiving him really as *man*. Let us illustrate what this means.

When a boy calls his girl "sweet," he calls her so as an existent subject. But he could also make her an "ingredient" of mechanics. He would do this by putting her on a scale. The scale says: "Ninety pounds," just as it would do if he had put a ninety-pound sack of salt on it. The scale cannot say: "Sweet." As "ingredients" of mechanics, girls are never sweet. In a similar way people are never religious as ingredients of the sciences.

The religious man, we said, sexually unites with another person and in his ecstasy he calls "God!" This is nonsense, of course, for anyone who makes sexuality merely an object of science. It is possible to describe sexual intercourse in terms of the working of certain glands, increase of blood pressure, a change in frequency, depth and volume of breathing —panting in ordinary language—etc. But one who thinks of sexual intercourse *only* in such terms had better not get married in church or even before a justice of the peace, for the only place where he belongs is in the laboratory.

"A child is born," we said, "and the believer exclaims 'God!'" That is why, soon after its birth, the child is carried to the temple or the church. This is done even if a child is stillborn. But if in an abortion clinic the physician kills the unborn child, it is simply dropped into the waste disposal unit. Things like this can happen only if the unborn child is reduced to a mere object of the sciences. In such a case nothing reveals itself of that mysterious "depth" which the religious man tries to express when he calls "God!"

For an understanding of existence as religious it is necessary that philosophy reject the services offered by the sciences, no matter how well-intentioned they may be. The religious man cannot occur in the sciences, just as "lovely girls" cannot occur in mechanics of physiology.

If this idea is accepted, one should cast a critical eye on the alacrity with which certain theological schools seek the support of the behavioral sciences as auxiliary disciplines for theology. For it is beyond dispute that the specific standpoint from which, e.g., sociology asks its questions excludes from its field of vision everything which theology tries to understand when it brings up the question of religious existence. Let us give an example.

A religious-sociological investigation recently asked the question: "Is the Bible for you God's Word?" About sixty percent of the people asked replied in the affirmative. *But no one knows what this statistic means.* The religious sociologist can communicate the result of his inquiry to the theologian. The latter, however, is not entitled to conclude from it that for sixty percent of the repliers the Bible is the Word of God. All he knows is that a certain percentage of repliers answered a certain kind of question in a certain way. That's all! He doesn't know *what they mean* with their affirmation. We should even add that the sociologist as sociologist doesn't know what he himself means when he asks others to answer this question. And if he thinks that he *does* know what he means with his question, then, as a sociologist, he still doesn't know whether he *rightly* means this. Thus I wonder how a theological school can build expectations on such a farce. "Science doesn't think" (Heidegger).

Calling the Name "God" and "Describing"

From the time when man began to think explicitly about himself, he has also tried to speak about the "depth," the mystery in his existence to which he gives expression when he calls the name "God." Sometimes he succeeded in this most ingeniously; there are not only geniuses in physical science and in ethics but also religious geniuses. The speaking of such geniuses enabled others also to "see" the "depth," the mystery in their own existence. It is this "seeing" which makes man call "God!" In ordinary language this "seeing" is called "believing."

Let's put full emphasis again on the term "calling." This calling may not be *replaced* by "flat descriptions," in which the name "God" becomes the subject of a judgment to which a predicate is ascribed. In other words, the calling of "God" may not be *replaced* by any statement like the following:

God gives us a child.
God restores my health.
God sends me an illness.

God has attached intense pleasure to sexual intercourse.
God makes the sun rise and set; he has placed the moon and the stars in the firmament.
God makes the sea roar, the wheat undulate, the storm break loose, the spring well up, and the seed germinate.
God gives us the victory in battle.
God inflicted a defeat on us.
God sends us poverty.
God has blessed me with wealth.
God permits that I suffer injustice.
God vindicates my right.
God intervenes in history.
God rewards the good.
God punishes evil.
God leads us out of Egypt.
God gives us possession of the land.
God gives us the Ten Commandments.
God leads us into exile.
God brings us back from exile.

The calling of the name "God," we said, may not be *replaced* by "flat descriptions" in which the name "God" becomes the subject of a judgment. We then presented a series of sentences in which such inadmissible judgments are made about God. But anyone knows that the believer, in whatever phase of history he lives, does make this kind of judgments about God. He expresses himself in the way which, we said, he should not use.

The Parable of Anthony Flew

The believer not only makes the name "God" the subject of judgments but also shows himself wholly impervious to everything that can be brought to bear against his statements. He behaves in this respect like one of the two explorers in Anthony Flew's parable. Flew speaks of two explorers who in the midst of a primeval forest discover a beautiful flower garden. "A gardener must have been at work here," says one of them. His companion doubts it, but is willing to take the necessary steps to verify the truth of the other's statement. In turn they mount guard at the garden, but no gardener appears. They dig a ditch around the flowers, surround the garden with barbed wire and an electric fence, and patrol the place with bloodhounds. Still no signs of a gardener. Not even once during the night do the bloodhounds stop and raise their ears; not even once does the electric fence record a contact. But the "believing" explorer is not at all dismayed by this. He finds it obvious that they don't perceive the gardener, for he is invisible; the barbed wire and the electric fence are useless in his eyes, for the gardener doesn't have a body; and that's also why the bloodhounds don't smell him, for he has no scent. Any facts put forward by his companion against his statement that a gardener must have been at work here, he simply disregards as irrelevant.

The believer is like this explorer. He says, "God gives us a child" or "God restores my health," but seems to remain unimpressed by what modern science tells him about the reproduction of man, health, sickness and death, fertility and lust. "God makes the sun rise and set," he says, even though he knows what the astrophysicist can say about the sun and how the meteorologist can predict when the sea will roar, the thunder roll and the sun shine. "God inflicted a defeat on us" or "God blesses us with wealth," he says, even though he is not unacquainted with the fact that strategists can explain victories and defeats and that economists can predict periods of poverty and of prosperity. The believer, the religious man, doesn't deny what the modern man of science tells him, but it doesn't seem to touch him in his faith. What does this mean?

No "Flat Descriptions"

This means that the believer *does not* conceive his statements, despite their external appearance of being statements "about" God, as "flat descriptions" of God's nature and actions. Despite the external appearance of his statements, he intends to express through them the "depth" of his existent subjectivity. The specific standpoint assumed by the modern sciences when they ask questions makes it *impossible* that the "depth" of human existence can appear before the eye of the modern man of science; that's why the believer can simply disregard the statements of these sciences as long as he himself in his seemingly "flat descriptions" does indeed intend to express the "depth" of his existent subjectivity.

But what happens if he does not, or does not any longer, intend this? What would happen if the believer begins to conceive his seemingly "flat descriptions" as really "flat descriptions," if he reifies or personifies "God"? Such a reification or personification occurs when the "believer," in saying "God gives me a child," "God makes a spring well up," God blesses me with wealth," "God makes the wheat undulate," or "God leads us out of Egypt," conceives God as a gynecologist, a geological factor, an economist, a meteorological factor or a revolutionary leader.

As soon as the "believer," the "religious" man, speaks about God as about a *thing* (a *res*) just as a geological layer is a thing, or speaks about God as a *person* just as George is a person, all sciences align themselves against him; for in such a case they are able to say *everything* that should be said. In other words, the "depth" of human existence is then no longer "seen," the "believer" has lost his faith, and there is every reason now to make only such statements as:

The gynecologist gives us a child.
A virus causes my illness.
The wind makes the wheat undulate.
Geological factors cause a spring to well up.
A stimulation of nerves causes lust.
Eisenhower gives us victory.
The government's economic policy brings us wealth or poverty.

Reification and personification are the great dangers of religious inauthenticity, which forever threatens all religiousness. Fortunately the rise and development of the sciences tend to make this danger increasingly smaller, for these sciences rightly point out the degenerations of religiousness which have occurred in the past and thus help prevent them in the future. This process of correction is known as "secularization."

"Every Dawn, Again, God Makes His Fiery Kite Rise above the Horizon"

Who still understands this language today, in our era of secularization? The fact that we must ask this question shows that secularization has also a darker side. There are indeed people who no longer understand such language precisely because it doesn't contain a "flat description." The absolutism of the sciences has led to a situation in which many people can understand only "flat descriptions" and have become insensitive to the meaning of the language by which the "depth," the mystery of human existence—God—is given expression. They no longer can read the religious writings of the past, preserved by the major religions, *because* the language of these writings is not a "flat description." The light of the sciences becomes an insuperable darkness as soon as it is absolutized. Let us use a comparative example to illustrate our point.

When a young man says his girl is "a peach," many people fortunately still understand his statement. But it is wholly unintelligible to anyone who is under the impression that the young man wishes to make a botanical statement. Obviously such a person would make himself ridiculous by claiming that the young man's statement *can* have only a botanical meaning and that he *therefore must* abstain from using it any longer. After all, don't we "modern people," living in an era of botanical progress, know much more than our ancestors about the structure, growth, evolution, etc. of peaches? One who argues this way doesn't understand anything at all of what that young man wishes to say. Similarly, what he really wishes to say he cannot express either in the categories and models used in the record of the psycho-technical testing which he and his girl friend once underwent.

"Old" and "New" Ways of Speaking "About" God

The believer's statements "about" God, which according to their external form establish, describe and explain, do not have a "flat descriptive" meaning. This idea is important for our endeavor to speak today "about" God better than formerly. Such an endeavor is essentially doomed to failure if one doesn't realize that any "new" way of speaking about God cannot have a "flat descriptive" meaning either. Let us list here a few statements which, according to certain authors, we may no longer use today:

God supplements my powerlessness in the world (Schillebeeckx).
God is my shepherd and Father (Harvey Cox).
God is the one who does something for me (Sölle).
God is a person (Robinson).
God is "above us" (Metz).
God is a powerful cause who, on occasion, must intervene (Walgrave).

According to the above-mentioned authors, we may no longer use these statements because we "modern men" have changed so much that statements "about" God coming from different times, different sociological conditions or different human situations can no longer tell us anything. Yet they wish to speak "about" God and therefore offer us other statements. Let us put their proposals down here in the same sequence as above:

God is the future of man (Schillebeeckx).
God is man's partner (Cox).
God is the one for whom I must do something (Sölle).
God is, by definition, the ultimate reality (Robinson).
God is "before us" (Metz).
God is the source from which we have the power to take our destiny in our own hands (Walgrave).

But these statements again must not be conceived as "flat descriptions." If one does it anyhow, they are no better than the old sequence. If, on the other hand, one does *not* conceive the old sequence of statements as "flat descriptions" of God's essence and actions, then one may legitimately ask whether they really are as bad as the above-mentioned authors seem to imply.

"Disclosure"-Situations

In what has been said until now we have tried to indicate the difference between situations for which "flat descriptions" are sufficient and others in which human existence discloses such a "depth" that the religious man is induced to call the name "God." It stands to reason that not all situations which cannot be covered by "flat descriptions" are religious situations. Outside the realm of the religious also it can happen that a situation suddenly discloses depth, that "the ice is broken," so that our "seeing" suddenly becomes different and demands a language which is more than a "flat description." Let us give two examples, borrowed with some modifications from Ian T. Ramsey.

A solemn reception is being held, let us say, by the Secretary of State on the occasion of the New Year. Not just anybody can enter there and partake of the cocktails and hors d'oeuvres. Invitations have been issued and accepted. Everyone is solemnly announced when he enters the hall. "Professor James Peterson, President of the United Gas Corporation, and his wife." Mr. Peterson strides forward; he doesn't walk, he strides. The ladies look to see whether his wife is again wearing the same dress she has already worn twice on previous occasions. A few formal words are exchanged, a few stereotyped wishes uttered. The boring ceremony goes on. "Mr. Peter Flynn, Chairman of Consolidated Gas and Oil." Another distinguished looking gentleman moves forward. The Secretary of State looks at him, he looks a second time, and then he sees it! Throwing both hands into the air, he exclaims, "Cookie!" He has recognized in the Chairman of Consolidated Gas and Oil a classmate from his school days, a boy who was rather shy and tended to remain aloof. During the lunch hour he would withdraw into the farthest corner and finish his meal with a few cookies. To avoid having to share his homemade cookies, he kept away from the others' company. That's why the others began to call him Cookie. And now he stands there before his classmate, the Secretary of State. As soon as the latter exclaims "Cookie!" the ice is broken, and when the other guests understand what has happened, the reception assumes a "merry depth." The language in which the boring ceremony could have been described until then suddenly becomes insufficient to express this incident.

Now for the second example. A judge handles routine matters, one case after the other in a monotonous sequence. Then a disheveled woman is led into the court; she is accused of perpetrating a swindle but, despite her appearance, one can still see that she has known better days. The judge looks at her record lying before him, pronounces her name, looks at her. Suddenly he blanches, stumbles over his own words and whispers, "Penny!" He has recognized in that unkempt woman before him his former wife, whom he had divorced some twenty years ago. After two years of marriage, he had gotten tired of her and embarked on a life of sin—at least that's what people used to call it at that time and it doesn't seem to me that today it should be called "the right thing to do." And now, all of a sudden, he is confronted with the consequences of his wantonness. "Penny!" That's what he had called her at their first encounter. She had dropped a penny and, while bending over to retrieve it, had lost her balance. He had managed to rescue her just in time from a nasty fall. That's the way it had all started, and now . . . he can only whisper, "Penny!" The entire court is deeply moved, as the newspapers report in detail. The judge withdraws from the case. The situation assumes a dramatic depth, and the language which the reporters used for the routine cases preceding this drama is suddenly insufficient to express what happened there between the judge and his wife.

These examples are offered here merely to illustrate that religious situations are situations in which a mysterious "depth" manifests itself. But the examples themselves do not specifically refer to a religious situation, but to another kind of "depth." To give expression to the religious "depth" which he sees, the believer calls the name "God." Even when he substitutes for this "calling" sentences which state, describe or explain something about God's essence and actions, *even then* the believer intends to express the "depth" of his own existence. Religious language is never a "flat descriptive language."

General Religiousness and Christian Faith

It is intentionally that we have not spoken directly about Christian religiousness and Christian faith because, with respect to the Christian faith and its language, we would like to put the emphasis somewhat differently than it used to be done by many until recently. In the preceding pages we described faith as a kind of "seeing," different from the superficial seeing attainable by anyone who has eyes or scientific methods enabling him to approach things and people in "flat descriptions." In Christianity, however, faith used to be placed *in opposition to* any form of "seeing." Faith was precisely *not* seeing; it was conceived as to admit "as true" without seeing.

And that which was admitted "as true" was a series of judgments, statements, "articles." These were directly or indirectly derived from Scripture, for the Bible contained divine revelation; it was what God himself had said about "divine reality." God's Word was assumed to contain secret information, for God's reality was called "supernatural" and therefore beyond the reach of man's natural vision. Supernatural faith, as a gift of God, enabled the Christian to accept that certain statements are *true,* that is, in harmony with the supernatural reality of God.

Moreover, under the influence of Greek philosophy this supernatural reality was represented as "reality"-in-itself, as a "reality" which, isolated and divorced from man and his history, simply is what it is, necessarily, universally, immutably and eternally "true"-in-itself. The truth of the "articles" of faith was conceived as their agreement with the "truth"-in-itself of divine "reality"-in-itself.

There was a time when this conception permeated the whole of Christian life as an "implicit option," an "unspoken assumption," something everyone accepted as a matter of course to such an extent that it did not even give rise to any question. Thus, when in the Middle Ages a theologian asserted that there are two persons in Christ and that in the Trinity there is one predicamental relation and two transcendental relations—today's reader doesn't even know what all this means—he was burned to death as a matter of course. In the perspective of the above-mentioned unspoken assumption prevailing in that stage of the Christian tradition, this consequence was indeed a matter of course. People then would say: "Look, this heretic will go to hell anyhow. Let's therefore give him a foretaste of hell fire while he is still alive. Let's tie him to the stake, so that he can experience something of what hell is before he is dead and while he is still capable of repentance."

That's why a priest was always close to the stake to absolve the wretched victim at the first sign of sorrow and repentance. People were convinced that in such a case they had saved a man from hell.

"He will go to hell anyhow!" This firm conviction was based on a presupposition, the assumption that belief is a yes to statements guaranteed by God himself. In medieval eyes, one who made assertions which were not in agreement with the information accepted as given by God himself about his own essence and actions could do this only because he proudly pretended to know more about God's essence and actions than does God himself. Such an insane pride would lead him to hell anyhow and therefore the stake was the last resort to save him.

The idea that faith must be conceived as a yes to information guaranteed by God and expressed in the form of judgments, statements and "articles"—that is, we think, the cause which has led Christians to a deathly crisis.

Faith as Accepting Certain Statements "as True"

When other people put "articles" of my faith before me, I feel rather ill at ease today. TIME's section on religion often contains paragraphs beginning with: "The Catholic believes that. . . ." People discussing issues sometimes say: "Catholics believe that. . . ." Let us complete the sentences and list some of the things which, according to others, are "articles" I believe in. Catholics believe that:

God created heaven and earth.
In God there is one nature and three persons
In Christ there are two natures and one person.
Man is born in original sin.
Through baptism man passes from spiritual death to life.
Mary was conceived without sin.
Jesus was virginally conceived.
Mary was assumed into heaven.
The Pope is infallible.

The list could be made much longer, of course. One who in the Catholic Church is called to a spiritual office must affirm these "points" and many others under oath.

It is *not* my intention to say that I do not affirm these points. But, suppose I didn't—what then? In asking the question, "Suppose that I did not believe these points, what then?" I understand the term "believe" in the interpretation which this term has gradually received in the Christian tradition; in other words, it is taken to mean a yes to *statements*. If, instead of saying a yes to these *sentences,* I were to say no, what then? What is the "importance" of a yes rather than a no?

Some people reply that the believer is certain of this "importance" because these statements contain truths guaranteed by God. As such, they simply *cannot* be without "importance." But such an answer merely postpones the question, for the conviction that God guarantees certain truths is itself also a matter of "faith." Once faith is reduced to man's yes to judgments, statements, and "articles," then the same must be said of the belief in the divine guarantee for the truth of certain statements. This "faith" then also becomes a yes to the statement, "God guarantees truth." But then the original question returns again: What is the "importance" of a yes rather than a no?

The Principal Difficulty

The main difficulty against the view that faith is a yes to statements has not even been named above. This objection lies in the idea that *no judgment, taken it itself,* tells man anything at all. A judgment *in itself* has no ground or foundation. Hence I never know "what a judgment is concerned with" if I have *only this judgment itself* at my disposal. That's why I can never say yes or no with respect to such a judgment. Let us give two examples.

I take an expensive cigar in my hand, hold my hand behind my back and tell a visitor: "This cigar is expensive." He can then neither affirm nor deny my statement. It has neither *ground* nor *foundation* for him; it doesn't *really* tell him anything; it doesn't express any *reality* for him. It would be just as foolish for him to say yes as to say no to my statement. And if he did it anyhow, his yes and his no would mean exactly the same—*nothing*. Divorced from the implicit "saying"-of-*is* which the existent subject himself is—in other words, divorced from the immediate presence of the subject to the reality disclosing itself—a statement has no *ground* or *foundation*. It is "not concerned with anything."

"To be sure," one may argue, "but who is going to ask aynone to affirm or deny such a statement?" I wouldn't do it, but what about the following statements: "God has created the world"; "God is all-powerful"; "God rewards the good"; "God punishes evil"; "God has become man"? It is not inconceivable that some people would pronounce an affirmation to such judgments. Others, on the contrary, would answer with a negation. Both, however, the affirmation and the negation to judgments, taken in themselves mean exactly the same—*nothing*.

This is the reason why the opinion polls in religious-sociological matters are so unimportant. The difficulty presents itself as soon as the questions have to be formulated. If these questions are borrowed from an antiquated handbook of theology, they frustrate the entire investigation from the very outset. But, let us suppose, the "right" questions are asked, whatever "right" may mean here. Even then they express, in the form of questions, judgments submitted to the respondents, to be answered with a "yes," "no" or "no opinion." When the results of such a religious-sociological inquiry are submitted to the theologian, does he really receive any information whatsoever about the *faith* of the respondents? The only person who can answer this question in the affirmative is one who starts with the assumption that faith is a yes to judgments.

Accordingly, when the newspapers report that

the opinion polls show again a decline in the number of people who believe in hell, then, theologically speaking, this means exactly the same as a reported increase in their number—*nothing at all.*

Let us add another example which will permit us to penetrate somewhat deeper into the original, implicit "saying"-of-*is* by virtue of which the explicit saying-of-*is* formulated in the judgment receives meaning. After a mountain hike I can give an objective description of the ease or the difficulty of the trail. This description contains a series of statements in which the passability or impassability of the trail is expressed by means of predicates. The statements which I make are explicit modes of saying-*is;* I explicitly ascribe certain predicates to the subject of the judgment and I do this by using the verbal copula "is." But if I present these statements to someone who doesn't know at all what is meant by a mountain and is also incapable of acquiring some understanding of what a mountain means, then my judgments about the passability or impassability of the mountain trail don't speak about anything to him. For me these statements speak of something because my feet and my hands, my eyes and even my entire body have already "affirmed" the passability or impassability of the trail. My walking, crawling and climbing, my tiredness, my discouragement, my scratches and my firm resolve to go on themselves are the "affirmation" of the trail. This "affirmation" presupposes an original "event," the "event" of a breaking through and transcending of the thinglike character of my being, the "birth" of the "saying"-of-*is* which subjectivity itself is. In a stone rolling down a mountain track no subjectivity "comes to pass." That's why the rolling of a stone over the path is entirely different from my rolling down the same path. I am the "affirmation" of the path. My subjectivity, immersed in my body, itself is the "saying"-of-*is* which I make explicit by expressing it in judgments. These judgments are preceded by the "event" of the coming about of meaning for the subject. My hiking over the mountain trail is fastened to the coming about of truth-as-unconcealedness. I can express this truth in judgments, but none of these has any meaning whatsoever if this truth is divorced from the "affirmation" which my existence is. Divorced from existence, a judgment is neither true nor false; it simply doesn't say anything.

This assertion applies to any judgment. In order to know what a judgment means, I must have more at my disposal than only this judgment itself. If this is not the case, then a judgment does not *say* anything. That's why faith cannot be conceived as a yes to a judgment taken by itself. Otherwise faith would be a yes to something which doesn't *say* anything.

Truth as Agreement

Above we have expressed our objections to one aspect of the interpretation of faith which has slowly penetrated in the tradition of Western thought, viz., the conviction that faith is a yes to judgments. The same tradition, however, also contains another unspoken option, a second "unquestioned presupposition," viz., the conviction that the *truth* of a statement of faith consists in the agreement of this statement with the divine "reality"-in-itself, that is to say, a reality which, divorced and isolated from man and his history, simply is what it is, necessarily, universally, immutably and eternally "true"-in-itself. If we refer to the first aspect of the Western interpretation of faith as intellectualism, the second can be suitably called objectivism.

Under the influence of Greek thought, this objectivism managed to dominate the West. Objectivistic thought separated and divorced not only supernatural reality but also natural reality from man; it conceived all reality as reality in-itself, as being what it is, even without man. The main difficulty which presented itself to the objectivist was the question how human knowledge could still be called *true* knowledge. For to be true, knowledge has to be in agreement with *reality*. But "reality" was conceived as "reality"-without-man, therefore also without human knowledge—in other words, "reality" that is not known. How could it be shown that "knowledge" agreed with not-known-"reality"? How could it be justified that a judgment agrees with a not-judged-"reality"?

To overcome this impasse, they had recourse to the hypothesis of substitute "cognitive images." Human knowledge was conceived as a mirroring-in-the-subject of a "reality"-divorced-from-the-subject by means of "images" which were supposed to be faithful "copies" of "reality"-in-itself.

This attempt, however, proved to be a failure. Whoever claims that knowledge is *true* because the knower is assumed to possess a copy of "reality" still must justify his claim that this "copy" is really a "copy." Now, a copy can only be called a copy when it is compared with the original and, on the basis of this comparison, judged to be faithful or an "accurate" copy. But such a "comparison" presupposes knowledge of the original—in other words, of reality. Once, however, knowledge is conceived as the "possession of a copy," the required comparison can be nothing but the comparison of a copy with a copy; in other words, the copy-character fails to find the required justification.

Accordingly, the objectivism contained in the

above-described conception of "reality" makes it wholly impossible for man to reach this "reality." This conclusion applies of course also to so-called supernatural, divine "reality." Once it is conceived as "reality"-in-itself, divine "reality" also becomes, as a matter of principle, unattainable for man. It is then a "reality" with which man, *as a matter of principle,* doesn't have anything to do. If, then, Revelation is presented as offering secret information about the divine "reality"-in-itself—and objectivism cannot take any other position—there can no longer be any implication that this Revelation is "important" for man. For, how could God reveal that man "has anything to do" with something which has already been "defined" as that with which man, *as a matter of principle,* doesn't have anything to do?

First Interlude: the Meaning of Presuppositions

The interpretation of the Christian faith which has become traditional, we said, can be described as a yes to statements which, on the basis of a divine guarantee, are judged to agree with a divine "reality"-in-itself. We did not say that any theologian has ever *expressed* the matter in such fashion. On the contrary, we would even be willing to accept the objection that *no one* has ever expressed himself in that way. But even if no one has ever *expressed* this, this doesn't mean that this interpretation has not always been *presupposed* as a matter *beyond question*. It is not so much what is said as what is tacitly presupposed that decides about the character, the fruitfulness and the future of a way of thinking.

Only later are the tacitly accepted presuppositions unearthed, put into question and subjected to criticism. This is what we witness today with respect to the Christian faith. It has caused a clear "division of minds." We would like to distinguish three groups of people in this matter.

First of all, there are those who simply refuse to ask critical questions about presuppositions. This means that they "steel" themselves in their "faith" and therefore are forced to accept as *essential* to Christian faith all their presuppositions, even if they are untenable. If others do ask questions about these presuppositions and think that they must be rejected, then these others are, in their eyes, *per se* "unbelievers." Such people cannot act as serious partners in a dialogue with those "unbelievers" because they refuse to reflect and hold that this refusal is an *essential* aspect of their faith. They like to say: "God himself has revealed this or that," but they refuse to ask what this means and don't realize that their very refusal itself presupposes a particular interpretation of "what this means" and that this interpretation could very well be extremely strange.

Second, there is a large group of people who ask "desperate" questions. The unquestioned character of their faith has been undermined and now they ask:

Did God create the world or not?
Does God love us or not?
Is God almighty or not?
Does God reward the good or not?
Did God become man or not?
Was Mary conceived without sin or not?
Is the Pope infallible or not?
Is there a hell or not?

They "desperately" ask for a yes or no. But no one

can speak such a yes or no without lapsing into the presupposition that faith is a yes to statements which, on the basis of a divine guarantee, are judged to agree with a divine "reality"-in-itself. Asked in this way, the questions cannot be answered because they presuppose intellectualism and objectivism. Yes and no would mean exactly the same here—*nothing* at all.

Finally, there are those who reject the intellectualism and objectivism contained in the traditional interpretation of the faith. I agree with this rejection and have already indicated why. But I cannot agree with the way many people who share this rejection express themselves. They say sometimes:

God did *not* create the world.
God does *not* love us.
God is *not* almighty.
God does *not* reward the good.
God did *not* become man.
Mary was *not* conceived without sin.
The Pope is *not* infallible.
There is *no* hell.

This is an irritating and especially a misleading way of speaking. It is misleading because it presents matters as if certain statements *per se* imply untenable presuppositions. It does happen, of course, that certain statements are badly interpreted. But is there any justification for merging such a bad interpretation with these statements and then denying them? Such a procedure is similar to defining the appendix as an infection, the heart as an infarct, a bone as broken, marriage as a running fight, and the psyche as a disturbance. Water is chemically defined as H_2O, and for a long time people took for granted that this was what water-in-itself is. When, subsequently, it was shown that such an objectivistic interpretation was untenable, would it have been right to express the rejection of objectivism by saying that water is *not* H_2O? Obviously not.

Second Interlude: the Infallibility of Statements

The topic of infallibility is under serious scrutiny in the Catholic Church at present. The issue is whether the pronouncements of the Pope in matters of faith are infallible and immutable *of themselves* or by virtue of the Church's unanimity. It strikes us that in this discussion the issue still appears to be concerned with the infallibility of *statements*. Faith, however, is *not* a matter of statements. But let us assume that infallible statements are possible, whatever this may mean. Even then, the understanding of what "infallibility" authentically means within authentic faith will require a foundation on a level of existence that lies deeper than the level of statements. For statements *in themselves* have no "ground"; both the affirmation and the negation of a statement *in itself*, even if this statement would be "infallible," mean exactly the same—*nothing*.

Third Interlude: the Implicit "Saying"-of-Is

The need to discover how it is possible to indicate a foundation or ground for any statement whatsoever finds expression in the imperative of contemporary philosophy: "Back to the things themselves" (Husserl). A statement doesn't have a foundation, and I don't know "what I am talking about" until I am *immediately* present to a reality appearing to me. The immediate *presence* of my subjectivity to a *present* reality is always presupposed by any statement, even when human knowledge is conceived as the "possession of representative cognitive images," judged to be copies of the reality. For, in order to justify the idea that these copies are truly copies of reality, the subject must be immediately present to the appearing reality. The subject, then, is "put outside himself," he "ec-sists," he is existent.

The existent subject is a certain "light." He is a "light" unto himself but also, as "put outside himself," a "light" in the world. The things in the world have meaning, "they tell me something" because by the "light" of subjectivity they have been drawn from concealedness. If there "were" only things, nothing would have meaning; the very term "is" would not be. No judgment whatsoever would then be possible, for in any judgment the terms "is" or "are" are used. Consequently, no judgment could then be *true*.

Accordingly, truth conceived as the agreement of the judgment with things has many presuppositions. It presupposes that the things are already *unconcealed,* that subjectivity as "light" has already emerged and that the explicit saying-of-*is* in the judgment is preceded by an implicit "saying"-of-*is*. The implicit "saying"-of-*is* is existence, that is, the subject as a "light placed outside himself." But reality can then no longer be conceived as "reality"-in-itself, divorced and isolated from the subject: on the contrary, reality "clings" to the implicit "saying"-of-*is* of existence. The explicit saying-of-*is* of the judgment or statement is based on the appearance of reality to the implicit "saying"-of-*is*. Divorced from this implicit "saying"-of-*is,* no judgment has any meaning whatsoever. The question which needs to be asked in our context is whether it is possible to execute a "return to the things themselves" to give a foundation to statements of faith. In our opinion, such a return is possible.

Christian Faith

We did not *start* this little work with an explanation of our objections to the intellectualism and objectivism which have infected the Christian faith in the course of the centuries. Intentionally that explanation was preceded by an attempt to interpret what is meant by "the religious man," the "believer." In this way we could at once turn away from the idea that the "believer" is someone who pronounces a "yes" to certain judgments; at the same time we could prepare an understanding of the idea that it is necessary to "return to the things themselves" with respect to the Christian faith by a partial execution of such a return with respect to the "religious man" in general.

The believer, we said, names, calls, whispers the name "God"; he expresses the "depth" of his existence thereby; the name "God" may not be made the subject of a judgment to which a predicate is added by the verbal copula "is"; the believer, we added, does this anyhow, and his insensitivity to anything that can be brought to bear against his statements shows that he doesn't conceive them as "flat descriptions" of God's essence and actions, even though his statements are cast in descriptive and explanatory forms. We interpreted man's general religiousness as a special way of "seeing," a "seeing" which is existence itself, and called this "seeing" man's "faith." The full emphasis in all this fell on man as *existence;* man should not be conceived here as an "ingredient" of "flat descriptive" sciences. Nothing of all this, we think, needs to be dropped when we try to interpret the Christian faith, but it will be necessary to make some additions.

"Christian faith presupposes revelation." What does this mean? The revelation which makes faith possible is a very special *way of life*. In the first instance this way of life was a reality in Jesus of Nazareth. He lived man's life in a special way before the eyes of his fellow men. Others saw this life and it was a "revelation" to them. They had never thought it possible for a man to live in such a way and now they saw it before their very eyes. That's why some began to "believe," that is to say, they also began to *live* in such a way. Their "faith" had been made possible by a "revelation," for if Jesus Christ had not shown them the possibility and reality of such a life, they would not have been able to live it.

Because the first Christians began to live like Jesus Christ, a "depth," a mystery revealed itself in their existence; and like Jesus, they expressed this "depth" by naming, calling and whispering the name "God." A way of life made it possible for them to shout "Father!"; and thereby they expressed the "depth," the mystery of their *new* existence. They realized that something special had happened to them, that this new way of life had, as it were, "descended upon them," that they had "received" it "from on high," and they exclaimed "God!"

Later some people replaced this *calling* of "God" by the statement: "God has revealed himself in Jesus Christ," but this statement obviously didn't have a "flat descriptive" meaning like the statement: "The President showed his hand through his Secretary of State."

The new existence is distinguished from the old one as freedom is from unfreedom, authenticity from inauthenticity, salvation from disaster, holiness from sin, life from death. A life in which man is a captive of pride, greed, lust, arbitrariness and unavailability is not-free, inauthentic, broken, filled with evil, sinful, and death. But when he accepts the new life, man "sees" that he is not the arbitrary lord and master of his new life, and in gratitude he calls "God!"

Later some people replaced this grateful *calling* of the name "God" by such judgments as:

God has freed us.
God has given us salvation.
God has renewed us.

But these judgments did not have the "flat descriptive" meaning that is suggested by their external form. They are not on a par with other judgments which externally resemble them, such as:
Eisenhower has freed us.

Peter has given us an apple.
The doctor has fixed me up.

In the light of their new life the first believers saw that their old life really meant nothing but death and sin. The realization that their new life had come to them "from above" disclosed a "depth" to them; and they expressed this "depth" by calling the name "God." Later this calling was replaced by statements containing a judgment. The first Christians said:

God has made us pass from death to life.
God has forgiven our sins.

But these judgments again did not have a "flat descriptive" meaning similar to the statements:

The teacher has made us pass from the fifth to the sixth grade.
The principal has remitted our penance.

Jesus of Nazareth revealed to man the possibility and reality of an authentic human life, but in doing this he himself became the victim of those who rejected this new way of life. But the first Christians realized that they, too, could have crucified Jesus if the new life had not been given to them. Jesus had become the victim of a way of living *which at one time had been also theirs*. And on the cross they heard him exclaim the name "God": "My God, my God, why hast thou forsaken me?" Yet they knew that a new, authentically human history had begun and in gratitude they called the name "God."

Later people again used judgments about all this, making God the subject of certain statements. They began to say:

God has put our guilt on Christ in order that he, who himself was without guilt, might expiate our guilt for us.
God has intervened in history.

But these statements did not have the "flat descriptive" meaning that is suggested by their external form and which makes them resemble such statements as:

The judge has condemned John, himself without guilt, to pay the debts of his neighbor.
The police have intervened in the rioting.

The people who wish to lead the life made possible by Jesus belong together and they come together. This is what we would like to call the "Church." They belong together because they share the same way of life; and they come together to call the name "God" in prayer, song, rejoicing, lament and sorrow. For they realize that they can never become lord and master of their own new life, that "what has come over them" must always again be given to them "from on high," that what once has been accomplished in them must over and over again be accomplished in them. Meanwhile they live in the conviction that their new life is "infallibly" good: "the Church of Christ is infallible."

Is this what the Fathers of Vatican Council I had in mind? We don't think so, but this is what they should have meant.

"I Believe in the Cross and the Resurrection of Jesus Christ"

What is the meaning of the statement: "I believe in the cross and the resurrection of Jesus Christ"? From the preceding considerations it should be clear that this means: I am willing to live, or at least I will try to live, as Jesus Christ has lived. It has no other meaning. If, then, I do *not* really wish to live so, I do *not* believe anything.

People who pursue various positive sciences could object and say: "As historians, we can prove, through the most reliable methods of the science of history, that Jesus died on the cross; through the medical sciences we can prove that Jesus was dead when he was taken down from the cross; moreover, we can prove that, medically speaking, he would have been asphyxiated, if he had still been alive, when he was buried wrapped up in one hundred pounds of myrrh and aloe-leaves; through the sciences of history we can also prove that three days later his grave was empty and that Jesus again discoursed with the living. All this has been absolutely established for us; therefore, we *believe*."

Those objectors would be right if faith should be reduced to a yes to statements made by the sciences of nature and of history. But this is not what faith is, and if faith is supposed to be this, then faith is impossible. One who merely executes an affirmation of scientific statements believes *nothing*.

Faith, as a yes to a *way of life,* has nothing to do with the modern sciences. Yet, "believers" in the past have gone to incredible troubles to *demonstrate* their "faith" scientifically. Consider, for example, the following statements:

Christ was virginally conceived.
Christ died.
Christ descended into hell.
Christ ascended to heaven.
Christ will return on the clouds.

Efforts were made to approach such statements with the aid of all kinds of scientific and historical considerations in the assumption that these statements were "flat descriptions" just like those of the physical and the historical sciences. But, we must ask, is such an assumption tenable? Mythical speech is *true* speech if it is understood according to its own intention. But mythical speech was understood as if it were scientific speech; and it became obvious that, understood in this way, mythical speech had to be called pseudo-scientific.

If faith in what "God has accomplished in Jesus Christ" were to demand of the scientist and the historian that they accept as scientific or historical truth something which, in the ordinary "course of affairs," is impossible to verify in the domain of physical and historical science, then "faith" becomes entirely impossible. In the pursuit of the sciences of nature and of history a certain "way of acting" is not only customary but also necessary if one is to speak of *truth* in the sense of physical science and of history. Scientific and historical truth imply a specific way of asking questions and giving answers, specific models, a specific use of language, etc. Without them there can be no question of scientific and historical truth. Now, it is inconceivable that the people who pursue these sciences impose these demands on their scientific pursuits on the one hand, and do not impose them on the other. But in the New Testament we constantly hear that God's action cuts across the causality occurring in nature and in history, while the phenomena related there cannot possibly be verified in the way this is usually done and has to be done in the sciences of nature and of history. Now, one who pursues a science cannot accept that specific laws govern the realm of his science and, at the same time, accept also that such laws from time to time do not govern the same realm. If, then, the "affirmation" of God were to demand of him that he accept as a scientific and historical truth something which cannot be verified by the sciences of nature and of history, then he could not possibly "affirm" God.

We have already indicated, however, that the "affirmation" of God doesn't make such a demand of him. On the contrary, we have even assumed that the pursuers of physical science and history could indeed prove all kinds of phenomena, such as the crucifixion and resurrection of Jesus; but we added that this wouldn't entitle them to think that they believe anything at all in the Christian sense of the term. The Christian faith has *nothing* whatsoever to do with the sciences of nature and history. Man is not a believer as an "ingredient" of the sciences or as a pursuer of the sciences. In the Christian sense, to believe in God doesn't mean to be able to "prove something," but to be willing to live like Jesus Christ lived.

"My Father Is Stronger than the Mayor"

Many people feel ill at ease when they encounter an attempt to disengage the language of faith from the "flat descriptions" of the sciences. This is understandable because we "modern men" have simply let ourselves become fascinated with the absolutism of the sciences. We are blinded by the "light" of scientific verification. How unreasonable this is may be illustrated by an example.

A twelve-year-old boy adores his father. He doesn't hide his admiration and is always boasting about his father to other boys. "My dad," he says, "is very strong. Why, he is stronger even than the mayor!" What that boy says is *true*. "Truth" here means the same as above when we said, "Myths are *true.*" They are true in what they *really* wish to say; they intend to express something which cannot be said in "flat descriptions."

If we were to listen to what certain authors writing about Jesus Christ say, we would be told: "That statement cannot simply be accepted. It must first be verified. So, we will have to put the boy's father in the ring together with the mayor; then we can verify whether what the boy says is true." To our mind, such an attitude is nonsense.

Sixty years later, the twelve-year-old boy has become an old man. Sitting on a bench in the park, he says to his brother who is two years younger than he: "You remember the fair in our village sixty years ago?" "Yes," replies the other. "And do you also remember how the mayor then stepped into the ring and challenged all passers-by to a wrestling match and how our dad took up the challenge and in no time had the mayor flat on the floor?" "Yes, I recall that, too." This story, too, is *true*.

But the above-mentioned authors, I fancy, will raise objections. They would say: "Let us, with the aid of the historical sciences, try to determine whether sixty years ago there was indeed a fair in that village. Next, let us try to establish whether there were reasons, whether economic or psychological, why the mayor could have been induced to strange ways of behaving. Finally, let us try to find witnesses and possible written documentation about the results of the mayor's wrestling. For only in this way can we verify the reliability and truth of what those two old men are saying."

This, too, is sheer nonsense. There is only one way thoroughly to falsify the truth of what that boy and those two old men said, and that is to accede to the demands of those authors.

Decades after the death of Jesus Christ, the first

Christians said to one another: "Do you still remember when. . . ." They wanted to speak about the Jesus who had taught them a new way of life, one which had made it possible for them to give up their pride, their greed, their lust, arbitrariness and unavailability. They wished to speak of the "depth" which this way of life had given to their existence, so that they were able to name, call and whisper the name "God." It is *this* that they wished to put down in writing, and not the things that could interest the pursuers of the physical and historical sciences. That's why they said: "Christ is the Word made flesh" and "Christ is God." And what they said was and is *true*. But their statements did not have and do not have a "flat descriptive" meaning as is the case with the statements: "Meat loaf is bread made flesh" and "Nixon is President."

"Definition" of the Contemporary Crisis of Faith

Faith, we said, cannot be defined as a yes to judgments, statements and "articles" which, on the basis of a divine guarantee, are taken to "agree" with the divine "reality"-in-itself. It follows therefore that the contemporary crisis of faith cannot be defined as a "desperate" uncertainty whether those statements "agree" with the divine "reality"-in-itself. The Christian faith is a way of life; hence a crisis in the Christian faith is a crisis in this way of life. And there is, we think, every reason to speak of a crisis here. This is manifest, for instance, in the decline of many religious orders and communities.

The Language of Faith

In the preceding pages we have repeatedly said that the language of faith is not a "flat descriptive" language. The statement "Christ rose from his grave" may not be put on a par with the statement, "Chris rose from his deck chair." If there is uncertainty whether or not Chris really rose from his deck chair, it is possible to send someone to verify whether he did rise from his chair. But if the one who went on this errand comes back with the news that "the deck chair of Chris is empty," it still is not certain that Chris really rose from his chair. It could have happened that his friends dragged him out of it unwillingly because in their opinion he had been lazing long enough in it. Thus one would have to search for reliable witnesses—preferably level-headed and unemotional people—who could testify that with their own eyes they saw Chris getting out of the deckchair. If one succeeds in this, then the statement is sufficiently verified to be acceptable.

If one claims that such a manner of verification is needed also in the case of the statement "Christ rose from his grave," then one places the two statements on a par. And this can be done only if the statement "Christ rose from his grave" is fundamentally misunderstood.

The "Self" of Religious Self-Understanding

The believer, we said, expresses the "depth" of his existence when he calls the name "God," and he does this even when he makes the name "God" the subject of a judgment. If this is so, then one can understand that "speaking about God is speaking about man." Unfortunately, it happens rather frequently that people conclude from this that *therefore* God is "really nothing," that is to say, "nothing in objectivity," but at most "something in man's subjectivity."

Those who represent this standpoint start from the presupposition that "something" is "something" only if it is either "something objective" or "something subjective." This presupposition dooms to failure their dialogue with those who say that a statement about God is a statement about man, for the latter precisely do not start from this presupposition. They do not work with the "model" of the divorce between the subjective and the objective but with that of the "reciprocal implication of subject and object."

If the "self" of which there is question in religious "self-understanding" is conceived as an "isolated" self, then one can justly maintain the accusation of subjectivism against anyone who admits that speaking about God is speaking about man. But, to-day, those who admit this certainly do not conceive the "self" or subjectivity as an isolated "self" or a "divorced" subjectivity. The believer's "self-understanding" is the self-understanding of an *existent* subject—in other words, a subject who is himself only in unity with what is not the subject, with the world, the body, God. Let us explain this a little more in detail by means of a few examples.

Regarding the things in the world, I can say that they are objectively "graspable." This means that they are graspable *for my hands,* and these hands should be "defined" as "I-who grasp." The fact that I have two hands and five fingers on each hand co-determines that things can be grasped in the way in which they actually can be grasped. If I had only one hand with only one finger, things would be graspable in an entirely different way. If the things in the world were full of protuberances and the human body were a ball, things would *not* be graspable. And anyone who claims, on the basis of those protuberances, that things would be graspable "in themselves" can do so only by mentally adding a couple of grasping hands to the ball. Accordingly, speaking about the graspable world is speaking about man. No form of subjectivism is involved in this.

If I am hot and thirsty, the water I drink is, of

course, no H_2O for me. Water is H_2O only when it is made the object of chemistry. One who claims that water *was* already H_2O presupposes that it *was* already an object of chemical considerations. In other words, speaking about the chemical world is speaking about man as a chemist.

When I walk around on a sunny afternoon smoking a cigar, I obviously do not have any white corpuscles in my blood. I have these corpuscles only when biologists make me the object of their science. One who claims that I *had* already white corpuscles in my blood presupposes that biologists *had already made* me the object of their studies. In other words, speaking about the biological world is speaking about man as a biologist.

All this means that the thesis "speaking about the world is speaking about man" should not be interpreted as if speaking about the world says "really nothing" about the world, but only says something about subjective contents. For subject "and" world constitute a unity of reciprocal implication.

It is not our intention to claim that the statement "speaking about God is speaking about man" is now clear. We have merely shown that the conclusion "God is 'really nothing'—i.e., 'nothing objective' but at most 'something subjective' "—is not valid. If I were to claim without any further ado that God is "something objective," I would give a "flat description" of God. Fertility and lust, health and sickness, the sun, the moon and the stars, the sea, a thunderstorm and a well, victories and defeats, poverty and wealth, justice and injustice, etc.—all these can be described as "something objective." But when this is done, there is no longer any reason to call the name "God."

We will return to this point after first quoting an appropriate text of Augustine in his *Confessions:*

> What do I love when I love You? Not bodily beauty, nor the fair harmony of time, nor the brilliance of light which gladdens our eyes, nor the sweet melodies of variegated songs, nor the fragrant smell of flowers, ointments and spices, not manna and honey, not limbs delightful to bodily embracements. None of these I love when I love my God. And yet I love a kind of light and melody, of fragrance and meat, a kind of embracement when I love my God: He is light and melody and fragrance and meat and embracement of my inner man, there where shines unto my soul that light which space doesn't contain, where resounds that melody which time doesn't carry away, where lingers that fragrance which the wind doesn't disperse, where clings that savor which eating doesn't diminish, and where is given that embrace which doesn't slacken through satiety. This is what I love when I love my God (*Confessions,* Bk. X, Ch. 6).

The Religious Use of Language and Criticism

If religious language cannot be called a "flat descriptive" language, the question must be asked whether this language cannot in any way be criticized. This question is urgent, for it is concerned with the issue whether there can be no way whatsoever of "verification" with respect to the religious use of language. In our opinion, religious language also must leave room for criticism, and there can and must be room for some kind of "verification." Let us first give a few examples which do not refer to religious language.

When the President says to someone: "I appoint you Secretary of State," he does not state and describe a fact or a condition, but he *performs* what he says. Because the language used is not "constative" and descriptive but "performative," the President's statement cannot, at least not primarily, be called "true" or "untrue." The same must be said if the President's daughter tells someone: "I appoint you Secretary of State." Such a statement is not primarily "true" or "untrue" but "successful" or "unsuccessful," "fortunate" or "unfortunate," "legal" or "void," "logical" or "illogical," etc.

One who investigates, however, why and when such a way of speaking succeeds or does not succeed meets facts that can be stated or conditions that can be described; and the statements about these facts or conditions can be called "true" or "untrue." Accordingly, a statement like "I appoint you Secretary of State" does include a constative and descriptive aspect, and this aspect reveals itself in the verification.

In a dormitory I suddenly hear the cry, "Fire!" This means, "Get out while you can" or "Stop doing what you are doing and rush to the aid of your fellow students." The cry's intention is not to state that the reality which an insurance policy defines as "fire" does as a matter of fact exist in the dormitory. The cry is not primarily "true" or "untrue." But here, too, the statement "Fire!" demands of necessity a certain critical checking or verification; and the result of this verification is a constative and descriptive statement which can be called "true" or "untrue."

If in a certain situation or at a certain meeting I become angry and shout "Damn it!" no one can reply: "Yes, that's true" or "No, that's not true." But what is possible is that someone will show me that the choice of my "language game" is not justified. He can show, for example, that I completely misunderstood the situation or misjudged the meaning of certain words. He does this by putting the "reality" and the "truth" of the situation or the meeting in a constative and descriptive language game, making me see that there was no justification for the language game I was using. My cursing was "not concerned with anything," for on closer inspection I saw that I stood in "unreality" and "untruth" with respect to the situation or the encounter which occasioned my curses. I apologize for my language game on the basis of a critical investigation into the "reality" and "truth" of the situation or encounter. This investigation is a kind of verification which discloses truth and untruth.

Hiking with a few friends through the country, we come to a simple inn where a crude sign announces: DINNER READY! The sign's intention is not to state and describe a fact or a situation. At home dinner is also often ready, but no one would think of hanging a sign in the window. If one of the children would secretly put such a sign in the window, he would be punished because he would be playing a language game which his mother has no intention of playing. The language of the sign is not primarily constative and descriptive but invitational.

If we enter the inn and we discover that dinner is not ready, the inn-keeper cannot excuse himself by saying: "Gentlemen, please! You should realize that the language of the sign is not constative and descriptive but invitational." For we could point out to him that he should exercise more caution in his use of invitational language. Knowing the tricks inn-keepers sometimes use to lure customers, my friends are not to blame if they first send me alone into the inn to verify whether dinner is really ready. Finding out that this is really the case, I return to my friends and in constative language communicate to them the results of my investigation, adding if necessary a description of the kind of dinner that is ready.

What these examples show is this: the use of language which is not primarily constative and descriptive, and consequently cannot be called primarily "true" or "untrue," nevertheless cannot place itself beyond every form of verification. A "moment" of "truth" or "untruth," a "moment" of "being about something" or "being about nothing" is always implied in such statements. The question, now, is whether the same must be asserted of religious language.

From Religious to Metaphysical Use of Language

A child is born, and the religious man exclaims "God!" No one can answer his shout by saying, "That isn't true." But this doesn't mean that no one can tell him: "Don't be so foolish!" The objector wishes to convey that this calling of the name "God" talks "about nothing." No one can dismiss this objection by saying that religious language is the language of praying and singing, lamenting, rejoicing and sorrowing, of binding oneself, hoping and despairing, etc., and that therefore it cannot be primarily called "true" or "untrue." One will have to show that precisely such language games are "about something." In other words, there must be room for a "critical resort" and for some form of "verification." For religious language also is exposed to "being foolish." It *can* suggest a "depth" that isn't there, it *can* point to a future that isn't really open. This means that the question about the "reality" and the "truth" of religious language imposes itself irresistibly; consequently also the question of a "critical resort" and some form of "verification" cannot be avoided.

This stands to reason, we think. For there is a kind of "religiousness" which leads people to sacrifice little children and burn widows, and another kind which contributes to the abolition of violence against humanity. There is a kind of "religiousness" which leads to temple prostitution, and another kind which invites to chastity. There is a kind of "religiousness" which functions as an opium of the people, and another kind which makes an authentic victory over despair possible. It can happen that "religiousness" is made possible by the development of physical science, but it can also happen that this development becomes the occasion on which religiousness finds its authentic expression. Certain forms of "religiousness" simply collapse when a political system comes to an end, and other forms save men by causing the downfall of a political system. Some forms of "religiousness" imply backwardness, ignorance, poverty, sickness, neglect of duty, intolerance, tyranny and psychical disturbances, and others foster man's discovery of authentic freedom. That's why there must be a "critical resort," an exercise of human "rationality," some form of "verification" with respect to religiousness. In the West this function has been exercised, and fruitfully exercised, by metaphysics.

The "Proof" of God's Existence

The core of that exercise of human rationality which is known as "metaphysics" is called the "proof" for the existence of God. The author knows, of course, that Kant subjected the traditional proofs for God's existence to a criticism which led him to reject them. For some people this meant that the matter was settled; thereafter they no longer wished to listen to any proofs for God's existence. But in philosophy nothing is ever settled. That's why others went to the trouble to determine *exactly* what Kant wished to reject when he allegedly rejected all proofs for God's existence. In the course of their inquiry it became evident that Kant didn't wish to accept any proof concluding to the existence of a God who was conceived as a sensitively given *object,* just as a geological layer, a cup, a toothbrush and a wig are objects given in sensitivity.

This point is now accepted rather generally. But the question that arose at this point was whether the ultimate intention of the traditional "proofs" for

God's existence was to show that God is a sensitively given object. If the "proofs," conceived as demonstrating that God is such an object, are not tenable, does it follow that they must be rejected *absolutely*?

It is easy to show that a "proof" for God's existence is not a "proof" if, with the aid of the physical sciences, it concludes that God is the first cause in a chain of physical causes. But if *such* a proof is meaningless, does it follow that every "proof" is devoid of all meaning? Gabriel Marcel answers in the affirmative, but is he right?

For Kierkegaard a "proof" for God's existence is simply shocking. In his eyes, God is the "most Beloved." Now, who would think of proving the existence of his Beloved "straight in his face"? Hasn't one who tries this already betrayed his Beloved? One cannot avoid asking the question whether the great metaphysicians of the past were ignorant of this. It hardly seems likely and therefore we must ask whether they really intended to prove the existence of their Beloved "straight to his face."

Heidegger simply observes that the traditional "proofs" for God's existence have never been able to do more than conclude to a God-Cause. But such a "God" is not for him a divine God. Who could pray to such a "God," sing or dance for him? Who could fall down on his knees in adoration for such a "God"?

These are the main contemporary objections to the "proofs" for God's existence. Obviously we do not intend to deny that the "proofs" have never been conceived in the way they are now so vehemently criticized. But even if in the past such a misconception actually did occur, this doesn't mean that the *proper* intention underlying the "construction" of a "proof" for God's existence must be rejected, together with those unfortunate ways of implementing the ultimate intention of metaphysical thinking "about" God.

The realization that the calling of the name "God" can be misleading has led *philosophers* to assume the position of a "critical resort" with respect to such "calling." For philosophy is "reserve personified." The politician lacks such a reserve when he issues his "call" and confesses his faith in a political program. But the philosopher as philosopher cannot possibly do so. His answer as a philosopher to the "calling" of the politician is always: "We will have a look." And then he critically proceeds to examine what is tenable and what is untenable in the offerings of the political program. But even if after his critical inquiry he thinks that he can agree with the program, he cannot take part in the "calling" of the politicians without ceasing to be a philosopher.

The believer calls the name "God" to express the "depth" of his existence. The philosopher answers: "We will have a look," and this means: we will try to determine whether this "depth" in human existence can be critically justified. But even if he succeeds in this attempt, it is impossible for him *as a philosopher* to pray to God, to sing and dance for him—just as it is impossible for a physicist *as a physicist* to call his wife "lovely." No one is entitled to blame him for this. One cannot blame silver for not being gold; yet there is every reason to value silver as silver even though it is not gold.

A Sketch of Metaphysical Speaking "About" God

Metaphysics dwells in "the wonder of all wonders" that there is something to "see" and something to "say." The most original "seeing" and the most fundamental "saying"-of-*is* is the existent subject himself. The subject is the "affirmation" of what is, of "being." This "affirmation" reaches being, and being appears to the "saying"-of-*is* which existence is.

The "saying"-of-*is* occurs on many levels; that's why there is question of "reality," of "being" on many levels. But this means that it is possible and necessary to ask about the meaning of *"the"* "saying-of-*is* and of *"the"* being which clings to and appears to *"the"* saying-of-*is*. *"The"* being is being *as* being and no longer as *this* being or *that* being.

Metaphysics asks, "Why is there something rather than nothing?" It thereby asks about "everything," but this term should not be understood as the sum total of chickens and eggs, cloud banks, courts of justice, stars and persons, but as the universality of being *as* being, the opposite of which is only nothing.

Of "everything" one can say that it is "something" and not "nothing."

"Why is there something?" This question asks about the origin of being, but it cannot be answered by pointing to a being among all beings as their origin. For, as a being, it itself precisely gives rise to the question about its origin.

"Nothing would be much more simple than being." It would indeed be much more simple if we could say that there is nothing and deny the "saying"-of-*is*. But this is impossible, for there is not nothing and the "saying"-of-*is* cannot be talked out of existence. Therefore, "The Other-than-being" ". . ." We leave the dots blank and refuse to say:

"The Other-than-being" is, exists.
The "Cause" of being is, exists.
The "Absolute" is, exists.
"God" is, exists.

Why do we refuse to say "is" here? Because "is" is what we say of all being. If I were "simply" to say that "The Other-than-being" *is*, I would lower "The Other-than-being" to the level of *being*.

We see here that the "saying"-of-*is* which human existence is, is not what it is without that "depth" in existence by which the affirmation of being is transcended. But the "saying"-of-*is* cannot be talked out of existence and therefore "The Other-than-being" ". . ." The refusal to replace the dots by "is" occurs in traditional metaphysics in the form of the recognition that the divine God ". . ." the Transcendent God. God does *not* appear as being appears because the divine God is *not* as being is.

There are many non-divine gods, but there "..." only one divine God, the God who "..." not, the God whose name cannot be made the subject of a judgment in which a predicate is added to this subject.

Nevertheless, as we saw, the believer makes the name "God" the subject of a judgment. This means that the believer runs the risk of falling into inauthenticity. In the past this risk was avoided by adding at once a denial to every affirmation made "about" the essence and action of God. One who formulates a judgment "about" God's essence and actions denies God if he conceives this judgment as a "flat description." The believer *calls* the name "God," the metaphysician *describes* the essence of *man* as a self-transcendent "saying"-of-*is*. No one, however, can describe God.

This is what metaphysics can "prove." But the possibility is thereby given to subject religiousness to critique, for any form of religiousness which affirms God as a being is inauthentic. That's why the metaphysician can tell the pseudo-religious man, "Don't be foolish" or "Don't be so mean."

"Don't be so mean," some "non"-believers say to others who would consider themselves believers. They say this when the latter—usually in good faith—make God the subject of a judgment and add to this subject a predicate which implies some form of "willing": "God wills this or that." Making such a judgment is not *per se* objectionable as long as the judgment is not conceived as a "flat description" of God's "will." But when the statement "God wills this or that" is conceived as a "flat description" of God's "will," then the content of this alleged divine "will" cannot be anything but the content of a human "will." One or the other form of man's "willing" is deified. Who, then, would be entitled to dispense himself from this "will"? Only one who can dispense himself from God's will—in other words, no one.

It cannot be denied, of course, that many forms of human "willing" are fruitful and humanizing in certain situations. But it can also happen that they become unfruitful or no longer fruitful because the situation has changed. And if under such conditions the statement "God wills this or that" is conceived as a "flat description" of God's "will," then this affirmation of "God" itself does violence to man.

"Good God! How Complicated Is Everything!"

That's the sigh heaved by many people who try to familiarize themselves somewhat with everything now being written about the faith and the "affirmation" of God. Too often these writings are not much more than intellectual gymnastics, but even when this is not the case that sigh is still appropriate, and perhaps even more so. The genuinely "great" religious thinking in the past and the present is indeed very difficult. Let us therefore dwell a little longer on this matter.

The Relative "Unimportance" of "Learning"

We use the term "learning" here in order to avoid the terms "reflection" and "rationality," which would require more explanations than "learning." What is meant by "learning" and a "learned man" is almost self-evident.

A simple man once told me: "One must have studied a lot to be stupid!" That's not true, of course, in every respect, but the statement can serve as an apt illustration showing that the level of "learning" occupies the second rank in comparison to authentic religious existence. This is true not only of religious existence but for all modes of existence. Let us give a few pertinent examples.

Anyone who is healthy can "intelligently" move around in space and time without any special difficulty. He "knows," then, what space and time are. But if we were to ask him, he wouldn't know the answer. And if he would try to define them anyhow, we could confront him with so many different definitions that he would quickly conclude that he doesn't know what space and time are.

But it doesn't trouble him at all. He doesn't know what space and time are, yet he knows how to move "intelligently" in space and time. Therefore, he *does* "know" them. *This* kind of "knowing" is a prerequisite for moving "intelligently" in space and time. And if at a given moment it becomes evident to me that my definitions of space and time are untenable, I have no reason to assume that I have *not* "intelligently" moved around in space and time. Implicit "knowledge," then, is important—of more importance than explicit rationality.

I encounter a high school student who has successfully finished his senior year. He would like to go to college and major in physical science. But a teacher has told him that "the professors" disagree about the definition of physical science. They wonder what exactly this kind of knowledge is and what conditions it presupposes. But they sharply disagree about the answer. We can safely assume that that student will never enter college to major in physical science if he makes it a condition that he first must personally understand the epistemological justification on which the possibility of physical science is based, for fear that he may be wasting his time in the pursuit of something that is impossible. And if by some miracle he would start his major in physical science anyhow, he would never finish it unless he gives up his self-imposed condition.

Other students act quite differently. They say: "I don't care one bit about the definition of physical science. And all epistemological disputes of 'professors' about the possibility of physical science be hanged as far as I am concerned. I am going to do whatever they call majoring in science for the next four years; and after that I'll know enough about the definition of physical science to pursue it." This is what we'd call a rational approach, the rationality of a certain form of "thoughtlessness."

If a young man and his girl do not wish to give themselves to each other in love unless they have first understood the essence of love and personally made its definition their own because they do not want to go "thoughtlessly" through life, they'll never even reach the first kiss. Other young men and their girls approach the matter quite differently. They simply try to do what "good people" call "loving each other." After ten years or so, they notice that it "works." And after twenty years they "know" what love is. But even then they are unable to define the essence of love if one asks them. It doesn't disconcert them at all.

Let us assume that I know the definition of prose. I am so delighted that I wish to explain the definition to someone else. And let us assume that my attempt succeeds, so that the other person understands my definition. How would he react?

If he has any sense of humor, he would say: "Imagine! I now realize that for the past fifty years I have been speaking prose without knowing what it is." Then, looking at me, he would say: "How is it possible to speak prose without knowing its definition?" My answer would have to be: "What you can do, to speak prose, is more important that what I can do, to define it."

An insight into the relative unimportance of explicit rationality is important also for faith. Last year, when I was preparing myself for the religious celebration of Christmas, someone asked me: "Don't you know *anything* about contemporary demythologization?" I indicated that I was not entirely ignorant of it, but I should have answered: "If some people who know *everything* about demythologization consider it nonetheless possible to celebrate Christmas with faith and piety, then I also know that people who reject this possibility know too little about demythologization to be entitled to talk about it."

But my parents and many other simple people know nothing about demythologization. Can they still believe today? They would not be able to do so if faith and explicit rationality were the same. For then one would have to find one's way through God knows how many theologies and find a standpoint from which all theologies can be evaluated. But faith and explicit rationality are not the same. Christian faith is a *way of life*, which theology "conceptualizes." It stands to reason that from the very start people have always been trying to do this, for whatever concerns us human beings remains alive only because we try to give expression to it. We keep talking about the fabulous achievements of Johnny Unitas because we want to keep them alive. It is partly because of our talking that Unitas *is* a famous football player; if the press, radio and television entered into a conspiracy of silence about him, our silence would reduce him to a mediocrity in the world of sports.

The first Christians gave verbal expression to their faith, their *way of life,* in order to keep this faith alive and spread it. Later people began to talk more and more about it. And in our days there is almost nothing but talk. Explicit rationality is at its apex, but at the same time it is also becoming very boring.

The relative unimportance of explicit rationality is strikingly illustrated by the *life* of simple good Christians. For example, these simple Christians do not declare a moratorium on the prayer of petition until "learned" professors can discourse meaningfully about it. When my mother offers a prayer of petition, a radical secularist would view her as a relic from a primitive period of history in which people were not yet able to help themselves and therefore had recourse to God. My mother sometimes prays for the success of one of my nieces' examinations. "Sheer magic," the secularist would say. But what happens when this niece fails miserably in her examination? My mother doesn't say: "What a swindle! It doesn't work." She simply goes on praying.

She doesn't need to make the meaning of the prayer of petition into a theoretical problem because, without the benefit of theology, she has long ago made the scholarly distinctions which thelogians laboriously try to put into words. She has "known" for ages that the prayer of petition is not an attempt to manipulate all kinds of intra-worldly causes, steering them into directions which on their own they would not "wish" to go. She "knows" that her prayer for my niece is not a request addressed to God to fill the gaps in my niece's knowledge or to suspend the psychological laws of forgetting things for a few days. Mother would not understand the theologians' claim that God has lost his "stop-gap function" in our secularized world because man has now come of age. As far as she is concerned, God can never lose that function because he never had it for her to begin with.

There are "believers" who swear that they will throw their "faith" overboard if "this" or "that" proves not to be true. By "this" or "that" they mean a particular theological view, statement or thesis. But what's the sense of such an attitude? To believe means to be ready to live in a certain way, the way Jesus Christ lived. Who could abandon such a way of life for the sake of a definition? Only one who confuses things that should not be confused. My ability to "move intelligently in space and time" does not collapse when my definition of space and time proves untenable and my "speaking in prose" doesn't become impossible when my definition of prose can no longer be maintained.

"Dinner Is Ready"

By way of conclusion, we would like to finish the example given above about the dinner that is ready to serve. It may be useful to some of my fellow believers, for they are "modern people" who like to verify things. For some of them verification has become a veritable passion, down to the ridiculous.

What can the inn-keeper expect when, after entering the inn to verify whether dinner is really ready, I return to my friends with an "affirmative description"? He expects, of course, that we will come in and have dinner. If we declare ourselves satisfied with verifying the inn-keeper's language and do not enter, we look like fools in his eyes.

We have the impression, however, that today many people are foolish in this way. They go in and out of any number of restaurants to verify whether the dinner is ready but appear unable to sit down anywhere to enjoy their meal quietly. They have a seeming excuse: they are "modern people," and as such they must pursue the positive sciences. They have to plan *scientific* models and techniques to verify whether dinner is ready. But while they animatedly discuss and argue about the nature of the models and techniques, they are wholly oblivious of the fact that others are already enjoying the meal.

Isn't there a contradiction in the fact that by means of the "thoughts" expressed in this little book we are trying to defend a certain form of "thoughtlessness"? Certainly not, at least not for one who put the emphasis on advocating only a *certain* form of "thoughtlessness."

Bibliography

Augustine, *Confessions.*

I. L. Austin, *How To Do Things with Words,* Cambridge, Mass., 1962.

A. I. Ayer, *Language, Truth and Logic,* London, 1953.

C. K. Barrett, *Jesus and the Gospel Tradition,* London, 1967.

P. Berger, *A Rumor of Angels,* New York, 1969.

W. T. Blackstone, *The Problem of Religious Language. The Impact of Contemporary Philosophical Analysis on the Question of Religious Knowledge,* Englewood Cliffs, N.J., 1963.

I. M. Bochenski, *The Logic of Religion,* New York, 1965.

R. Bultmann, "Neues Testament und Mythologie," *Kerygma und Mythos,* I, 1960, pp. 14-48.

———, "Zum Problem der Entmythologisierung," *ibid.,* I and VI-1.

———, *Glauben und Verstehen,* II, Tübingen, 1961.

———, *Jesus Christus und die Mythologie,* Hamburg, 1964.

T. P. Burke, *The Word in History,* New York, 1966.

N. Clarck, *Interpreting the Resurrection,* London, 1967.

J. B. Cobb, *Living Options in Protestant Theology. A Survey of Methods,* Philadelphia, 1962.

Harvey Cox, *The Secular City,* London, 1967.

I. M. Connolly, *Human History and the World of God. The Christian Meaning of History in Contemporary Thought,* New York, 1965.

A. de Waelhens, "Signification de la Phénoménologie," *Diogène,* No. 5 (1954), pp. 49-70.

Leslie Dewart, *The Future of Belief. Theism in a World Come of Age,* London, 1967.

Mircea Eliade, *Aspects du Mythe,* Paris, 1963.

D. D. Evans, *The Logic of Self-Involvement,* London, 1963.

Jacques Ellul, "Mythes Modernes," *Diogène,* No. 23 (1958), pp. 22-49.

A. Farrer, *The Glass of Vision,* Westminster, Md., 1948.

A. Flew and A. McIntyre, *New Essays in Philosophical Theology,* London, 1958.

F. Ferré, *Language, Logic and God,* New York, 1961.

G. Gusdorf, *Mythe et Métaphysique,* Paris 1953.

———, *Traité de Métaphysique,* Paris, 1956.

Martin Heidegger, *Being and Time,* New York, 1962.

———, "On The Essence of Truth," *Existence and Being,* London, 1949.

———, *Holzwege,* Frankfurt a.M., 1963.

———, *Was ist Metaphysik?,* Frankfurt a.M. 1955.

———, *Essays in Metaphysics,* New York, 1960.

———, *Vorträge und Aufsätze,* Pfullingen, 1954.

———, *Gelassenheit,* Pfullingen, 1959.

———, *Nietzsche,* Pfullingen 1961.

C. G. Hemple, "Problems and Changes in the Empiricist Criterion of Meaning," *Revue internationale de Philosophie,* IV (1950), pp. 41-63.

John Hick, *The Existence of God,* New York, 1964.

Edmund Husserl, *The Crisis of European Sciences and Transcendental Phenomenology,* Evanston, Ill., 1970.

Immanuel Kant, *Critique of Pure Reason.*

Ludwig Landgrebe, *Philosophie der Gegenwart,* Bonn, 1962.

W. A. Luijpen and H. J. Koren, *Religion and Atheism,* Pittsburgh, Pa., 1971.

J. Macquarrie, "Religious Language and Recent Analytical Philosophy," *Concilium,* Vol. 46 (1969), pp. 159-174.

———, *God-Talk. An Examination of the Language and Logic of Theology,* London, 1967.

A. McIntyre and P. Ricoeur, *The Religious Significance of Atheism,* New York, 1969.

Maurice Merleau-Ponty, *Sense and Non-sense,* Evanston, Ill. 1964.

———, *In Praise of Philosophy,* Evanston, Ill., 1963.

J. Moltmann and J. Weisbach, *Two Studies in the Theology of Bonhoeffer,* New York, 1967.

M. Müller, *Sein und Geist,* Tübingen, 1949.

———, *Existenzphilosophie im geistigen Leben der Gegenwart,* Heidelberg, 1949.

S. Ogden, "The Christian Proclamation of God to Men of the So-called 'Atheistic Age,'" *Concilium,* Vol. 16 (1966), pp. 89-98.

———, *Christ Without Myth,* New York, 1961.

———, *The Reality of God,* London, 1967.

Thomas Ogletree, *The Death of God Controversy,* New York, 1966.

R. Pettazzoni, *Essays on the History of Religion,* Leiden, 1954.

O. Pöggeler, *Der Denkweg Martin Heideggers,* Pfullingen, 1963.

I. T. Ramsey, *Christian Discourse. Some Logical Explorations,* London, 1965.

———, *Prospects for Metaphysics. Essays of Metaphysical Exploration,* London, 1961.

W. J. Richardson, *Heidegger. Through Phenomenology to Thought,* The Hague, 1963.

John A. T. Robinson, *Honest to God*, London, 1963.

———, *Exploration into God*. London, 1967.

———, and David L. Edwards, *The Honest to God Debate,* London, 1963.

Mortz Schlick, *Gesammelte Aufsätze,* Hildesheim, 1969.

Walter Schulz, *Der Gott der neuzeitliche Metaphysik,* Pfullingen, 1957.

N. Smart, *Reasons and Faiths. An Investigation of Religious Discourse, Christian and Non-Christian,* London, 1958.

F. Theunis, "Prolegomena zum Problem der Entmythologisierung," *Kerygma und Mythos,* VI-1.

Paul Tillich, *Systematic Theology,* 3 vols. in one, Chicago, 1967.

Paul van Buren, *The Secular Meaning of the Gospel,* London, 1963.

A. Vergote, "Mythe, croyance aliénée et foi théologale," *Mythe et Foi,* aux soins de E. Castelli, Paris, 1966, pp. 161-194.

F. Waismann, "Logische Analyse des Wahrscheinlichkeitsbegriff," *Erkenntnis,* I (1930), pp. 228-248.

J. Wisdom, *Philosophy and Psycho-analysis,* Oxford, 1953.

Ludwig Wittgenstein, *Philosophical Investigations,* New York, 1953.

H. Zahrnt, *Die Sache mit Gott. Die protestantische Theologie im 20. Jahrhundert,* Munich, 1967.

W. F. Zuurdeeg, *An Analytical Philosophy of Religion,* London, 1959.